Building Sales Warriors: Mastering the art of hardcore sales generation

Paul Clark

Clink Street

London | New York

Published by Clink Street Publishing 2017

Copyright © 2017

First edition.

ISBN:
978-1-912262-16-8 - paperback
978-1-912262-17-5 - ebook

Introduction

My name is Paul Clark, a sales person with 11 years B2B sales experience, selling in a highly niche and lucrative media sector from which we would bring buyers and sellers together to engage in the right environment in order to help them achieve their goals. We specialised in selling to C level decision makers from companies as large as IBM, SAP and Microsoft, from industries all over the world. Finance, Telco, Oil and Gas, Marketing… BLAH, BLAH, BLAH. Stop, hold the phone, let's get something really clear and from the outset. The products or company I worked for don't matter. I am not going to bore you with *'Hi my name is'* absolute slim shady bull****… *I sold this much… I'm this good, Blow me…* #BSW is about the real and raw approach to selling. I want this book to be honest and about a clear-cut approach, and a simple system that can go from an idea, or a simple paper-based lead, to money in your pocket. Not only that, I'm going to show you everything from understanding your customer, creating the Sales Warrior funnel, to closing like a BOSS in ten really simple steps.

So is this book for you? I've no idea… Whether you're a CEO or senior business leader who wants to help increase sales standards and pipeline in your business, or you are a newly appointed sales executive fresh out of Uni, I literally have no idea if this book is right for you… The reason I don't know is I don't know who you are. Whether you have it in you and you have what it takes to be a truly successful Sales Warrior. It takes something special for someone to become a Sales Warrior. Something that I will define in Stage 1 of the book. So read on and find out. If you can guarantee after Stage 1 you tick all the boxes, then read on because I have created a system that if mastered correctly can create you incredible amounts of sales, smash your targets out the sky and help you become seriously wealthy. BUT this is not for the faint-hearted; you need to fit the mould. Because this system will NOT work unless YOU are 100% committed to each stage of mastering the art of hardcore sales generation.

Like I say, I don't know if this is for you and I'm not expecting anything, but let me promise you this – if you make it to Stage 10 then you could be one of the very few that make it in becoming a true Sales Warrior. One of whom can blow the rest of your peers and competitors out of the water. And most importantly achieve your upmost desires and whys…

Welcome on board – this is your ticket to long-term success, BUT ONLY IF YOU HAVE WHAT IT TAKES TO TAKE IT FORWARD.

STAGE 1

Are you a Sales Warrior?

I know what you're thinking... I'm on to Stage 1, let's see what this so-called sales guy has to offer, and how can he make me a what do you call it?? So-called Sales Warrior?? Or here we go again another salesman thinking he has the keys to the kingdom with another sales book that I will either not understand or agree with and chuck in the bin??

Scepticism, just like any buyer would have. So it's totally understandable, but you have bought the book and you have read through to Stage 1 so the door is open. So it's very much like a sell you would make. Why have you continued so far?? The same reason anyone would, we are all searching for ways we can sell more and make large amounts of money and change our lives for the better. Agreed? Good. Well then that's the first box checked in becoming a Sales Warrior.

We all need to have a reason. A reason to want to increase the amount we sell and a reason to want to push ourselves. And when I say push ourselves, I mean stretching beyond what our mind currently thinks is enough.

We naturally have an ability to settle for what we currently think is pushing ourselves, but you would not be reading this book if you didn't want to improve. You need to take yourself to a whole new level of work-rate and stretching, in order to break barriers in becoming a Sales Warrior. Nothing worth having comes easy, so you need to firstly be prepared to take yourself to a whole new level of work-rate.

THE REASON ALL SALES FAIL WITH THE SALES WARRIOR CONCEPT IS THEY ARE NOT PREPARED TO WORK HARD ENOUGH AND DO WHAT IT TAKES.

Once again I'll say it, I don't know you and who you are and what kind of person you are. BUT you absolutely need to get this right from the off. If you are not prepared to take yourself to a whole new level of pushing yourself, then you will never make this work and you should throw the book in the bin NOW. As it's as good as done. Very few have mastered my concept but the people that have went on to be incredibly successful and wealthy. Again, this is about you not me or anyone else. So if you're ready and agree then continue reading.

There are two types of sales people in the world for me – 'Cruisers' and 'Drivers'.

Cruisers will be the ones typically with money in the bank, ok with just plodding along doing the odd deal here and there to hit their number and hit their quota. Just cruising against the average or amicable performance number. But also, Cruisers will look back and use their previous performance as a reason for why they can cruise and why they can work less hard. I've heard every excuse under the sun from Cruisers. They are not poor performers but they are not ever going to be Warriors and break boundaries in their performance and achieve their vision.

Then there are 'Drivers'. Drivers, typically, are characters that are always pushing and pushing hard to hit their numbers and sometimes a Driver typically would be a new starter learning the job, who has the hunger and desire to strive on for success. A Driver would work harder than everyone else, never settle for less than perfection. But gives it everything. And the key to a really good Driver – they don't stop once they hit their number and get to what the business they work for is considered a suitable a high-performance; for example, just hitting their target. A Driver keeps on pushing past it and determines their own level of excellence. That, my friends, is a true Sales Warrior character.

Now it's important to mention, whether you're a Cruiser or a Driver it doesn't matter. Being either, you still need to push past the threshold. As for me, it is easy to be a Driver, get some success, then sit back and become a Cruiser. I see it all the time, and it's the biggest failing of a talented sales staff. Whether it's that you hit a rut, just lose rhythm, confidence or simply a lack of enthusiasm. I'm going to give you a tool to help you move right past that.

It's not easy to just suddenly push yourself that extra yard without reason. You have to understand the things that drive you. Goals are performance markers, and achieve you short-term success, and yes, if you keep setting goals, then you keep performing and hitting those goals. But to be honest shaping a goal is difficult, because we say to ourselves *I want to buy a house*, *I want to buy a car*, material shit. But if those are goals that drive you then so be it.

But to become a Sales Warrior you need to build and write a picture of your future, paint that picture in your mind, and create a mental photo of what it looks like. A picture built from your emotions and a picture built from what improving your performance to a whole new level will give you.

And do you know what, don't hold back!! Make that picture exactly what you would want as a dream, because your new found success is going to make that dream a reality.

Now, you have the work-rate and commitment to push yourself to a place with no limits. You have a picture-painted vision of your reason to reach new heights, but you need one more thing... Making sure you are in the right role with the right company but, most importantly, the right product.

No matter what, the Sales Warrior concept can get you success in anything you do and whatever you sell, BUT for you personally the product has to be right. Only for your benefit. I was lucky to sell something in my career that was fantastic, and that's why when I created the system it brought me incredible wealth and success. But I also met and worked with people who came from companies that were selling absolute horseshit products, and to be honest it's like pushing that shit up a hill with a rake. Do yourself a favour – if the product is not good, well, how you can expect to sell enough to the volumes I'm going to be asking for later in the book with a shit product?

You need to be confident with what you're selling and that will only come if you're happy with the product. If you're not, get out and find the right company. Now whether there are alarm bells ringing or not, that's up to you. If they are, then they are for the right reason (you love what you're selling), or the wrong reason (you hate what your selling) – this will make no difference to the outcome of you becoming Sales Warrior, but you will never reach your full potential.

If all these points are aligned then congratulations, ya filthy animal, your internship begins for becoming a Sales Warrior.

STAGE 2

Understanding the Buyer and your Personal Persona

People say Telesales is a dying art. People prefer face to face. No one wants an unsolicited approach. It's all about the consultative approach…

All this may or may not be valid, but who knows??? Really??? The fact of the matter is that there are two minimum in a boss-to-boss conversation between a sell and a purchase. Obviously if there are multiple people involved, then that grows, but if you are targeting the right person – the decision maker – and you are providing the right solution which can help them, then it's a very simple process that I will explain step by step in this book. Because there is no ONE way of selling and persuading people to buy from you. To be honest the keys are determined by the buyer at the point of purchase, and where they sit against their purchase threshold. What position are they in to buy? Are they in the market for your solution right now? Are they natural buyers and like to buy, or have they had a lifetime of bad or negative purchases that have made them sceptical about purchasing anything ever… or do they simply have the budget lying around and need to spend it.

The one thing we can determine here is an understanding of who your buyer is and what they are looking to achieve; what kind of buyer they are; and how they want or wish to spend. This is completely out of your upfront control before your first initial contact, whether that be an email, phone call or knock on the door, but in the conversation or at least opening the conversation you can discover what kind of buyer they are before you proceed to pitch them on whatever solution you have. This is imperative and explained in Stage 7 of the book.

Two things you need to learn first – the two keys to success which will move you on your path to becoming a Sales Warrior.

1 – The client needs to understand that your product or company can help them achieve their goals or objectives.

2 - You are likeable and overall credible business leader who the customer would want to work with.

Whether you think these two seem obvious or not, these two points are biblical to the BSW concept. In order to open the door and build a conversation, the customer needs to tick these two points off in their mind to ensure that you are not wasting their time, and you have a genuine opportunity that can help them achieve their goals.

This is the Holy Grail for me. And what a rush as well. Getting a cold contact from somebody that you have never before spoken to, and within 30 seconds of the contact the buyer thinks you are **credible** and someone that can **help them achieve their goals**.

How do I get these two points, I hear my trainee warriors ask??? Hold ya horses everyone, watch me whip and watch me neh, neh. You are about to learn the BSW sales funnel… But read the Holy Grail again on my two points of what a buyer really wants from you. Once that is lodged in your mind you can't lose, and you're on your way to making a deal, as long as you follow every other Stage provided…. Bounce on to Stage 3.

STAGE 3
The BSW Funnel – your Ticket to Success

Ok, hold my beer….

I'm going to get all sentimental and writer-author, and tell you a little story. I'll keep it short, bit like me.

When I started as a sales guy I had NO idea what the fuck I was doing! Like… at all man!! I was employed in publishing and selling advertisement space, but literally had no idea on how I could take a lead and turn that to cash in my hand. Nobody really explained it to me in simple terms. People just said this is the area you are selling; let's say for examples sake, GARDENING. So all the product suppliers that provide gardening equipment would be the companies I would target for advertising. Simple, hey? Yeah, it's simple, but to be honest there is a whole lot of shit that goes with being able to transfer a company name that provides SHOVELS or SPADES on a website, to money in MY pocket. Questions like, what companies do I target?? What person within that company is the right person to target?? How do I manage that process of multiple decision makers and influencers?? How do I engage the customer? Deal with objections? How do I sell and not present? How do I ask the right questions to uncover need? How do I close hard as hell, and with confidence to get the decision to sign up? ETC… ETC… ETC…

Fact of the matter is nobody had really shown me a process of achieving ONE deal, in terms of stages of a deal for me, and what that looks like.

So I mastered a process for myself which showed me five steps of how to go from lead to deal. This process is THE MONEY, because once you understand how the 5 steps of your own sales process and cycle works and looks, and you master them, then you can increase the volumes to a level which is completely limitless, but for your own personal abilities. Now this comes back to *Stage 1 - are you a Sales Warrior?* The setup of the sales BSW funnel is simple, and I wish someone had taught it to me when I started, as this would have saved me years of learning by myself and making lots of errors, which would have helped me get rich quicker. GOOD NEWS FOR

YOU – for the simple cost of this book, you have skipped years of poor training and time wasted, waiting until some sales guy decides he's going to give you the keys to the kingdom. Well congratulations it's yours – and you have my word, you get it right then you can consider that painting of what your future looks like – ROMEO DONE… Thank me later.

So here it goes.

Think of your normal sales funnel and create it with 5 very simple blocks. As you see below, it starts wider and gets thinner, until you get to the point of the funnel which gets you to the deal. Now these are stages from start to finish of how your daily process would look like and how your own personal stages of the pipeline look. So you can always be in control. The most important thing is VOLUME. If you can achieve mastering the below process, layered with volumes in each stage, then you will master the art of the BSW sales funnel. I have formula I stick to, which I will give to you and which is your target point. But to be honest, the higher the volumes and output at the top of the funnel, the more opportunity that is going to be created that will constitute you doing more deals.

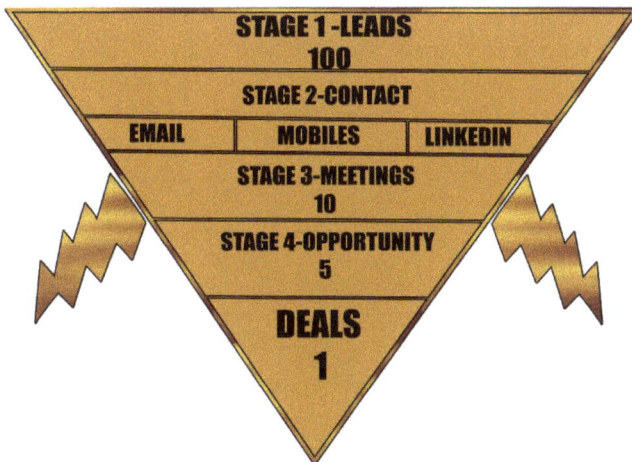

STAGE 1 -LEADS
100

STAGE 2-CONTACT

EMAIL | MOBILES | LINKEDIN

STAGE 3-MEETINGS
10

STAGE 4-OPPORTUNITY
5

DEALS
1

What is absolutely key with the BSW funnel is that it's all about volumes as I said before – the key to consistent and successful sales success in your control.

1. Having the warrior mentality and work-rate
2. Having a clear system from lead to deal
3. Understanding what volumes/numbers you need in each stage to be able to achieve your number (target)

A good company will give you a set of key performance indicators (KPIs) to hit, but a lot of companies won't. KPIs can be tarnished with the wrong brush. From my experience as a senior business leader, the term KPI can be looked at as numbers by which senior management can push and manage performance. This is true, but to be honest you only need to worry about YOU. If you are selling and smashing targets that's all that matters, right?? WRONG. The BSW funnel is your personal machine to be able to break barriers in performance. As mentioned in *Stage 1 - are you a Sales Warrior?*, you need become a Driver, pushing and focusing on your picture of success and striving to that goal. The BSW sales funnel can shoot you past the high-performance barrier and into your own league.

In media sales, for sponsorship I used **100** leads in my bank at start of sales campaign, backed up by as many contacts possible to decision makers – from those leads to be able create **10** meetings in my diary per week which would then create **5** opportunities per week, which would lead to **1** deal. To do a £12,000–£20,000 new business average deal a week in the media game was unheard of, but I managed it using this method.

Once we read on I explain Leads, Contacts and Meetings and Opportunities in more depth, which will make it a lot easier for you to determine your BSW funnel numbers. So don't worry too much, all will become clear.

The BSW funnel is applicable to anything you sell. You just need to focus on the volumes and output, starting from the top and working your way down. Eventually, once you master the system, you can become unconsciously competent at the BSW process relating to the 'unconscious competence' learning model from which the end result you can do it easily without even noticing you're doing it.

So that's the BSW funnel. It's really that simple but it's the MONEY built with your warrior mentality and your understanding of how to visualise your reasons and motivation. You now have the framework to build incredible sales success. Now I'm going to break each stage of the funnel so you can master how to work your funnel correctly, with impeccable results and CASH MONEY.

STAGE 4
Lead Generation and who to Target

Leads are the first part of your funnel. The widest, and of course being the first, the most important. All stages of the BSW funnel are important. But above all the reason leads is the widest is because you need a lot of them!!! Now the trick is to utilise every single one. And I'll teach you how, but to start with, whilst you work your system and get competent with it, keep that baby full at the top of the funnel.

Whether you're a recruiter looking for candidates, sponsorship sales, software, or a field sales team selling charity donations, it doesn't matter you, have to put yourself in a position to have enough leads in front of you or around you to be able to create enough activity around those, in order to engage them and move down the funnel.

Understanding who your GOOD lead bases are is absolutely essential! Let me throw down some examples. You need to build a landscape of what an ideal client would looks like, someone that needs your product, or someone that's in the market for your technology. Similar companies or prospects that have booked with you before, for example. Whatever you are selling you have to know your audience and understand who you are targeting. Name, company, job title, are all absolutely key. But for me the essential is 'know your customer', and find out something that is going to impress them – that added extra piece of research shows that you have gone the extra mile to understand their business needs, and shows you care and that you are truly interested in helping them. A new product launch, an award they won, a recent acquisition. It's all about knowing your customer.

Organise your leads in a simple way that can help you drive the work-rate against the lead base. Simple, easy to arrange, easy to use and easy to work. Whether you use paper based leads, a notepad or an Excel spreadsheet, it doesn't matter, but what's essential is you are happy with it and its ease to work with, from lead to lead.

You may have a CRM, if so get them organised into a campaign format, with everything you need in one place at one time. But if not, for example, I set my leads in a simple format which details everything I need to work fast. Everything I need is there at my fingertips. What's paramount now is managing that lead base so you can drip every lead dry. Too many salespeople churn through leads and pass over a lead because the lead isn't picking up the phone or has not replied to the email. The fact of the matter is the ones that don't come back to you reply are often the ones that will book with you, or part with their money. You just need to do something different – a new approach and a fresh outlook. A Sales Warrior thinks outside the box. A true Sales Warrior will take every single lead at his disposal and ensure that they book or blow, every single one. This is a massive lesson in the path of the Sales Warrior! DON'T CHURN LEADS, YOU WASTER… The reason is, the most difficult of leads I have had have often been the ones that booked! The problem with the sales world is most people are looking for the easy wins and are not prepared to put the graft in to get the results – see Stage 1 of your training, are you a warrior? Warriors don't look for easy wins, easy wins are just wins, the same as the most difficult of opportunities to turn over are just wins. And once you get a win, you're on to the next lead and the next one.

Your leads are your ammunition, your tools. Imagine a box of nails – they are your leads and you are the hammer about to smash them in. If those nails ain't sharp then they ain't going to go in.

So to recap; leads, you need lots of them. Let's say for the benefit of the BSW funnel you start with 100. Then you need to create your spreadsheet or system of manging those leads, and you need all the data you need there in that place, so you can work hard and fast against your lead base. Don't churn and waste leads. Work every single damn one until they book or blow. It's not about the easy wins, it's about dripping every lead dry so that your volumes are higher and your return in deals reflects that.

The key thing about your leads is the person or contact you are reaching out to. It needs to be the right contact, you need to know exactly the right person you need to contact, or what we call the decision maker or person of power.

Once you have identified the right person from each of your leads, it's time to engage!

STAGE 5
Engagement, your Voice is your Instrument

Congratulations! You are on the path to becoming a Sales Warrior. The ability to engage with people is the skillset that will differ you from all the average sales joeys out there. I've seen some ridiculous approaches in my years – robotic, monotone, bland and just genuinely fucking boring! Sometimes I don't know why people even bother going into sales when they come at it with such a lifeless and unenthusiastic approach. The fact of the matter is, folks, people buy off people. This is an important lesson in building a warrior's approach to sales. It's all about that connection between you and the customer. They need to absolutely love you before they even know anything about your product.

The reason being, you are asking them to part from their hard-earned cash. Whether it's money they have saved, or just budget they have put aside for the right project. Without that personal connection and rapport with the customer, you have no chance of selling them anything or at least if you do get the opportunity to pitch them your offering, the customer isn't really with you, because they don't believe or trust you. Sounds harsh but it's true, and it's a consistent mistake in sales, more often than not.

An example from past experience; I had a sales member who was an absolute warrior on the phone. Smashed his KPIs out the park and worked harder than anyone else on the floor. He was creating lots of opportunities, but they continued to blow out and not percolate into business. Even when I jumped on the back of the next step – the call back to take the conversation forward – it was gone. Lots of smokescreens and just a genuine blasé approach of not wanting to move ahead with the deal. When I reviewed his calls, I noticed a real passiveness to his tone, a sort of disinterest at the front end. Asking questions without any real feeling or care, and then just proceeding with the call in order to get to the end. We made changes instantly and for the sake of explanation we will go through some of the most important parts of engagement, and using your voice as an instrument in order to pitch with empathy, passion and pace.

Think of the pitch as a journey – for instance think of the most beautiful trip you have ever been on. Perhaps if you're a cyclist, or you have been on a nice holiday somewhere, or if you have been on a long hike, walk or something (these are all things I personally would never do BTW!) But have you ever said to yourself 'oh my husband or wife would love this' or 'I wish my mate was here to see this with me'. Then think about that conversation you have with them about the trip or journey you had. You want to paint them a picture like they are there with you.

It's like telling a story, and you want that story to be perfect. Every little emotion and feeling you had, and the detail of what the best parts of the journey were. Cutting through all the bullshit for example 'I was walking along a dull grey path for 15 miles to the top of hill, the view was great' to 'There was this incredible winding path that grew narrow around curving hill and then the view from the top was just amazing, it really was breath-taking, you could see everything'. I can imagine right now the in monologue, reading those two back to you, and I guarantee the first you read slow, dull and boring and the second you read with passion, belief and empathy.

They say on a pitch over the phone is 93% tonality and 7% words, and also face to face, 55% body language, 38% the tone of your voice and then 7% words.

To be honest what is apparent from my perspective is tone, and that your voice is your instrument. There is lots of training around pacing – so speeding up and slowing down your pitch to make it exciting. Mirroring – mirroring the personality of the person you're pitching to; example if they are slow and bit laid back, don't come in fast and excitable, mirror their exact tone and match their pace of conversation.

These are all important practices for using your voice as an instrument. But for me, sales is natural, even the dullest of people when they tell a story of something they are really passionate about come to life! So it's a practice I swear by.

It's all first about building a great story (your pitch) and ensuring that you're taking them on the same journey as you, and you're with them all the way. Watching out every single thing you say to ensure they are on that path with you.

So, putting it into product terms, you have to absolutely love what you do and believe in your heart that your product is amazing. If you don't, as I said at the start, get out and find the right one! The beauty of REAL sales and being a Sales Warrior is I teach people to sell as a REAL person, not pretend nonsense. No car salesman stuff here guys. You need to be happy with what you are selling. If you BELIEVE in your product you will believe in your pitch, and clients will believe you and your product.

I can train you on how to be passionate and empathetic, but these are natural abilities that come if you believe in what your selling. They are not things that are taught. They are inside of you, because I guarantee you have told that one story to a colleague, friend and loved one and their eyes lit up, because they were there with you and that's because you painted picture.

The major thing for me in terms of engagement is qualification. The qualification of the customer to let you have a REAL conversation or set up a meeting to pitch your product. The customer needs to love you and understand that you can help them and you're not going to waste their time. So the absolute importance of first-time engagement whether it is a cold call or an email setting up an appointment. The customer needs to know:

- You are credible
- You're not going to waste their time
- And you can help them achieve their goals

So these are the BSW three points of engagement, and are a big part of the warrior mindset. It's the go-to for any engagement you make. And if you master the three over and over again on every first-time engagement, you will win more conversations.

Hers is an example;

Hi my name is John Smith,
I am the Sales Director for Company A

I apologise coming in unannounced but I wanted to reach out reference to your fruit and veg business. I was really impressed with regards to your company's set up, and I think the brand looks outstanding.

I have a large number of contacts in your space that would be extremely beneficial to your current business and growth plans.

I would really appreciate jumping on a call or setingt up a meeting face to face, as I believe I have a number of ways that I can help you achieve your current business objectives.

Is there a suitable time we could connect?

John

This is an example. But to break it down, the first part is about you and your business. Clearly stating with strength and authority, this is who I am, and this is my company.

Then you move into your reason, so quickly getting to the point, so as not to waffle and waste their time. Clearly getting across that you are really impressed by their business, and stating clearly towards the end you may be able to help them and their business.

Then closure for the meeting, and getting that all important appointment set (this will become more apparent in the next stage of the book). You always leave an open question, so they have to answer there and then. For example, don't put 'please reach out if you feel it would be suitable'. Don't give the power back to them to decide. You need to ask them for the opportunity for you to engage in conversation, in what will be a connected and closed-door opportunity for you and the customer. You need them to qualify YOU for an opportunity, for you to pitch them.

Now, to the Holy Grail of Build Sales Warriors.....

STAGE 6
Scheduling Meetings

Scheduled meetings and appointment setting is the absolute key to Build Sales Warriors. I call it the Holy Grail because if you have got across in your first touch engagement, you are credible and you are someone who is not going to waste their time and you can help them grow their business. You have done something that will make your life easier… Notice that through my book there is no subject on objections, the reason being is I don't believe in them. Especially smokescreens – it's a load of crap! Smokecreen objections, for example *I'm not interested* (before they even know what it is), *send me and email, we have done this before, we don't use these types of services,* they are all signs that you have not been qualified by the customer to pitch them and you have moved ahead without them believing that you are credible, someone that's not going to waste their time and help them with their objectives. Also – quite painful – they don't really like you. Smokescreens are quite offensive ways of just getting you off the phone or out the door. That why the engagement part of BSW is so important.

The beauty of setting up meetings and appointments is it eliminates all smokescreen objections because he or she has already qualified you for the call. The only thing they can give you now are real objections (questions) that help you build relationships and move the conversation forward to ensure there is a fit for both parties, which is exactly where you want to be!

What do you do if you get a smokescreen during your first touch engagement my future warriors ask?? Simple, you go back to the BSW three points of engagement:
- You are credible
- You're not going to waste their time
- And you can help them achieve their goals

This is to be repeated to the customer until blue in the face, more determined than ever. As long as you believe in yourself and you believe in your product you will get the appointment and opportunity to pitch.

There are multiple ways of scheduling appointments but the key is getting your first touch engagement message to them, and there are multiple ways of doing this. This comes back to the BSW funnel.

Stage 2 of the funnel is **contact**, which shows the following three parts: emails, mobiles, LinkedIn. These are what I like to call your engagement or contact behaviours. These are the areas you work through on your lead base, touching every single one, across every contact. This is where you work the shit out of your leads.

To your decision maker or target there is a process of gates to that contact if you can't simply knock on their door in their office. I have created this diagram for you based on a high end C level approach. It may be lower for you but you can always take some of the gates away if you don't have them.

Decision Maker | Mobile | DirectLine | Linkedin | Email | Secretary

The decision maker is the target far left and each gate has an access point to that contact and this is one of your opportunities to engage with the customer. The closest being of course their mobile, followed by their direct line, LinkedIn, Email and Secretary.

Let's run through each gate and how best to maximise them.

Mobile – Obviously for any of your contacts on your CRM or your leadbase you have created. If you have the desired mobile/cell phone of the prospect, then you are more likely than any of the other gates to get the contact on the phone, which is the goal right?! If you can get the business or mobile phone of your target prospect then you are going to be able to schedule more meetings quickly and at a volume that will see you hit the number of meetings the warrior funnel demands. But if not its ok, because you have four other gates you can explore to contact your prospect.

Direct line – This is the same as mobile apart from the fact that people are spending more time out and on the road than they are just sat in their office expecting your calls. But it's another option for you to use and an important gate to explore and gain contact

LinkedIn – Social media has become an incredibly powerful sales tool over the years and LinkedIn is now the go-to social media platform for business, but it's also extremely good for connecting and first time engagement with potential prospects. You need to create a written copy of your engagement pitch which I have given you as an example, and you can use this as a means of sending personal messages and or LinkedIn Inmails to your targets prospects.

Email – The same as above for LinkedIn. Use your targeted engagement mail to send to your target contacts as a means for getting their engagement

Secretaries and receptionists - This is important to me but I want to be clear. They are also called gatekeepers by some people. To be honest they are very important and unlike other sales people I have a different approach. People try to bullshit them and blag their way through to the target prospect but secretaries and PA's need to be treated with respect as they are paid to stop idiots getting through to their boss so that people don't waste his or her time. Because believe me a majority of the time that's what's happening. The prospect is being bombarded by constant calls of bother by people trying to pitch their products to them. So differentiate yourself from all the other Muppets and utilize the secretary by using your engagement message and asking them to relay the message to their boss. Use and utilize them to help set up the call.

So as you can see there are multiple gates of engagement first touch with a target prospect from your leads. The cardinal sin of most salespeople is they smash the hell out of one gate over and over again. Why, I don't know… I can only assume they haven't been taught the above system to explore other ways to the target prospect. OR, for example, this complete nonsense that cold calling is dead and it's all about the social sell. What a load of horseshit! People that say that are usually the people that are not capable of it, or don't have the skillsets to be able to approach over the phone or cold call. People lean to the social approach as it's easier, with less conflict or rejection because it can be simply ignored. The fact of the matter is a Sales Warrior will approach, and become skilled across, all entry points to your contact. And you need to consistently work through every gate over and over until you book or blow the prospect.

This is why the organisation of your leads and contacts is key, as you want to tick off each gate on each of your leads to ensure that you have tried every approach, until the customer books or blows.

I will say this to you now loud and clear: if you practice the art of quality engagement around the BSW three points:

- You are credible
- You're not going to waste their time
- And you can help them achieve their goals

And you work against your target list of 100 leads and contacts using the engagement practice I have provided with a clear message that supports BSW three points of example:

Hi my name is John Smith,

I am the Sales Director for Company A

I apologise coming in unannounced but I wanted to reach out reference to your Fruit & Veg business. I was really impressed In regards to your companies set up and I think the brand looks outstanding.

I have a large number of contacts in your space that would be extremely beneficial to your current business and growth plans.

I would really appreciate to jump on a call or set up a meeting face to face as I believe I have a number of ways that I can help you achieve your current business objectives.

Is there a suitable time we could connect?

John

And you drive that message straight through every gate of contact to your target prospect as per below working and ticking off every single one as you go you will create huge volumes of engagement and maximise the potential number of meetings you can schedule in the funnel.

Decision Maker ⎰**Mobile** ⎰**DirectLine** ⎰**Linkedin** ⎰**Email** ⎰**Secretary**

The final thing for you to do is focus on the volumes of appointments/meetings you target per week.

I have a rule that says that every five proposals you send out to target prospects after a pitch should convert to a **minimum** of one deal. Giving yourself some wiggle room for meetings that cancel or roll over to the week after. I say the number which is stretching yourself to ensure you finish each week with five proposals out and one deal per week. You need to target volumes of ten scheduled appointments/meetings per week.

As you can see Building Sales Warriors is about a lot of the work that goes into the front end. My theory is that majority of your work is creating enough potential opportunity for you to pitch. The key for a Sales Warrior is volumes. The goals for anyone is that you want to be pitching your product all the time to potential customers, right? Well this system will give you the opportunity to set that up. Then the rest is in your hands: keeping on top your number and focusing on those all-important ten meetings per week.

Now this is not easy. I did and scored deals back to back, week in week out for 12 weeks until I was promoted and started teaching others to do it. There are not many people out there that have the guts and drive to make the system work. But if you do success and wealth is right round the corner.

A little advice –

RE: Voicemails, as this will come up. Always leave a voicemail otherwise it comes across as an odd approach. Go back to your BSW 3 points of engagement and get that across confident and close out for them to give you a call back or you will give them a call back and try again.

RE: Emails/LinkedIn always send in a three-pronged approach over the course of one week if you get a consistent 'no reply'.

1ˢᵗ approach - Normal outreach is written around your 3 points,

2nd approach – 'Not sure you got my last message' repeat of your normal outreach to follow,

3rd & final approach – 'Sorry I must have the wrong person please could you recommend the right person to connect with.

STAGE 7
Questioning, Understanding Needs & Building Real Rapport

The BSW approach is a numbers game. The more you push into the top of the funnel then the more opportunity you have of deals to come out the back end. The key for you is appointment setting with high volumes. It is hard graft but once you have that customer locked in for the meeting then there is a formula you need to stick to with every pitch you make which will make your pitch easier and more engaging.

The goal is to get them at the front end to love you all over again, like they did the first time. And it's about delivering… yep you guessed it! The BSW three points of engagement!

- You are credible
- You're not going to waste their time
- And you can help them achieve their goals

Now I'm not going to go through on how to pitch product as that's the easy part! You should all know how to pitch your product but the key is when the time is right and that comes after:

- You have questioned them to understand clearly who they are, what they do and what their product is
- Have a complete understanding of their personal and business goals and objectives
- Built REAL rapport from which you have connection with the customer who believes that you can help them.

When you master this process you will know when the time is right to deliver your pitch: it's when you have created what is called the deal baby. When you understand what their challenge is, matched with your product, that creates the solution.

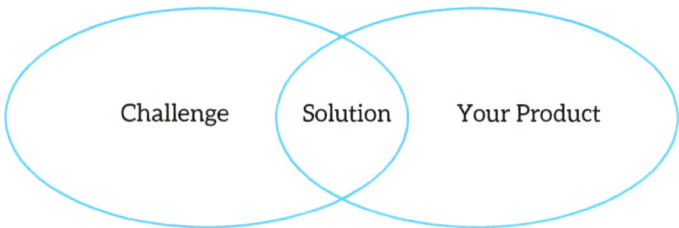

Challenge   Solution   Your Product

So in order to create a deal baby you have to question intently, with a clear goal of outcomes to follow.

All questions will differ depending on your product and offering. But my biggest piece of advice is be overly curious about their product and just as excited as they are, but don't pretend to know what they do better than them – just be with them in their journey of explanation.

At the same time, you don't want to question off the topic or direction of your personal goal of the pitch, which is to close the sale. Be goal-oriented and always ask questions that move the conversation forward to you being able to pitch the product.

There are two things that come of good questioning right at the front end:

- You are showing an interest in to them, their company and that you want to understand clearly what is their biggest challenge, so you can help them achieve their goal
- By doing the above you build REAL rapport and create a relationship sell

Questions should be constructed as follows:

Priority Question Number 1 – getting a clear understanding of who they are and what they do

Example: "Now before I dive in to what I do as a business, I am REALLY keen to learn a bit more about you and your business, and importantly what your product and value proposition is to the market?"

This gives the customer an opportunity to talk about their product and much like you, they love their product and believe in it. So, this is a great way to get your customer in a nice place and positive mindset, which is a position of sale.

Now, you may want to ask more questions about the product which is great, and if you know the industry then crack on but beware. There is a danger zone in which you are not an expert and he or she is. You are an expert of your product, so let them be an expert of theirs. You will have your chance to shine but the key is making yourself super-curious, and always having a goal-oriented approach to what's next to move that conversation forward.

Priority Question Number 2 – How does that link in to their personal and business goals and objectives?

Example: "Fantastic! So how are you approaching the market and what are the goals and objectives to getting that proposition to the right people?"

You are now looking to understand how they need to get to their target market and audience and what they need as a solution to help them overcome their current challenges and meet their objectives.

Priority Questions Number 3 – What will success look like to them and what would business be worth to them in terms of value?

Example: "What will success look like to YOU and the company and what would business be worth to them in terms of value?"

You want to understand what success looks like to them as result of getting business. Clear understanding of what they price so that you can price accordingly and present the right offer aligned to them.

Questioning is about gaining a real understanding of what they really want and how you can help them. Now, really important, a pen and piece of paper are your best friend at this stage. You should be taking down every single word they say because this information will be how you create that alignment with the customer and how you go about creating your deal baby, an offering that will provide a solution to help them achieve their goals.

There are three rules for questioning you should stick by:

- Let them talk, don't interrupt. This is their chance to feel like they are in control and let them walk themselves towards the next stage of your pitch. Don't rush them as you are building rapport, and your pitch is moving progressively and elegantly along in the direction you want it too.
- Listen intently, complete silence until you are ready for your next question, and take notes.
- Be over-curious; ask questions with interest, care and excitement.

Get the client into a position or buying threshold from which your pitch is welcome, and clearly shows that you can provide a solution to the challenges they explained, and you can help them. It's extremely powerful, as you are letting them bring to the surface on their own what the problems and pains are, so in effect they are doing a lot of the pitch for you. Then when the time is right they are ready to hear how you can help them. Then you're ready to pitch your solution.

Now, there is a really powerful tool to use here which sets up your pitch nicely, and just creates that exciting platform from which you're saying, *right you have had your time, it's my chance to show you how I can help*. Credit Jordan Belfort, who has always been an influence of mine in sales, but I have put a name to this technique, as it's a good way to set up the pitch conversation and also for you it's a marker in terms of where you need to get to in your pitch to move forward.

I call it your 'lever', and I use a JB line for this. "Ok great, so listen John, from what you have just said I think my product and offering is going to be absolutely perfect for you." Then you proceed with your pitch.

Now the beauty of this is, and you will notice this exactly if you follow the BSW process and you get to this point in the conversation, but you have not been given a smokescreen yet… And 100% at this point you won't. That's the beauty of the Sales Warrior concept – you have more time having engaging, valuable conversations than beating your head up against the wall while someone tries to kick you out the door or put the phone down on you.

What is great is now that you're in your pitch presentation you will get REAL objections (questions and buying signals). Now an important lesson here is not to plough through your pitch to the end and slam them for a close, just to get an opportunity created in your pipeline. This is a fatal error in sales. People gravitate towards volumes so much that they plough through pitches without slowing down and, most importantly, welcoming each and every question, good or bad, the customer has.

The key here my young warriors, the goal, is by the end of your pitch you have that all-important agreement between you and the customer to move forward for the deal, or to a next step conversation with a desired outcome.

You have to welcome all questions, good or bad. As in sales, your job is to understand and appreciate their position, and provide them with solutions. To persuade them in the right way that it's the right opportunity.

Salespeople are tarnished with a bad brush because there are really poor oversellers out there that care only about the deal and their back pocket. So, whatever you do, if you're not in a position where eye meets eye you must walk away. There is nothing wrong with that, and it will happen. Move on to your next target and have an agreement to stay in touch.

But to understand where the deal is at, you must constantly welcome questions and queries and overcome them, and agree with the customer to move on in the pitch or presentation.

If it's a bad objection then the key is to be not to conflict with it, but treat the question with respect and dignity. Not to be hostile. Appreciate, differentiate, and ask questions to get to the root of that problem. Really get to know why the customer has given you that question, as 90% of the time it comes from a bad experience and their buying belief. So, in order to get round the toughest of questions, you need to build rapport with the customer to understand the root of that problem, then elegantly overcome it.

If it's a good question buying signal – don't start getting hyper-excited but calmly appreciate it and continue elegantly with your pitch. I've seen salespeople, over the years, halfway into the pitch, get the customer saying they are interested in moving ahead, and go straight to cost! You have to continue forward elegantly and build value, stay on track and finish the job. It will continue to build value although they may have more questions.

As mentioned by the end of the conversation the only things you want to question on are the following:

- What is the cost?
- Do they need to speak to anyone else for a decision?
- Is the timing right for them?

Be thorough, be curious and listen intently. Questioning correctly whether giving or answering is the absolute key to finding that perfect point between the customer and you in order to close the sale.

STAGE 8
Creating Opportunities & Managing the DMP (Decision Making Process)

So the final stage in the BSW Sales Funnel is Opportunities. As mentioned previously, volume is the lifeblood of the BSW warpath. It's what sorts the men from the boys, the women from the girls. But you would not be this far in if you didn't have what it takes, so good on you.

We discussed the following, but let's have another quick look at the funnel to remind ourselves:

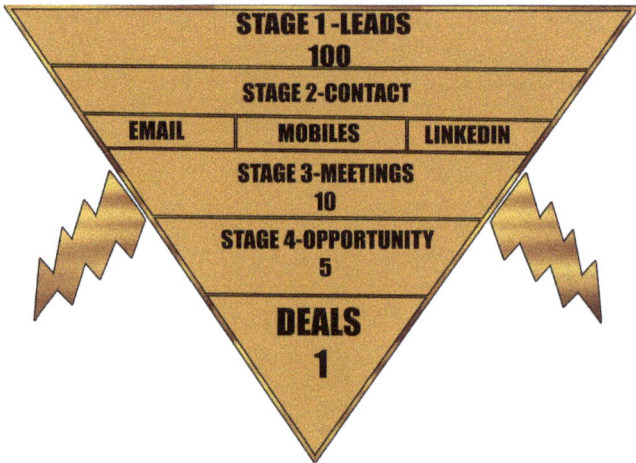

Ten scheduled meetings/appointments per week will give you a conversion of meetings to opportunities of 50%. You may convert more which is great, but the minimum result for you will be that you can create five opportunities per week.

What is an opportunity? It's an agreement between you and the customer to move forward to either deal, next step conversation or to speak with another person within their organisation.

This is a critical point in decision making. Now I don't know what you're selling but if you are selling to just one person then that's great. But I'd say a majority of the time people will ask for other people within their circle or business for advice on moving forward.

The key is to gather an understanding no matter what of what that looks like, and manage that process if you can, to support progressing the deal forward.

We are in a difficult time financially globally, some more than others, but in this day and age people want to spread the risk and share responsibility with others so that if it goes wrong it's split responsibility, not just on the buyer's shoulders.

This is one theory, but also you may be speaking to an influencer of the decision maker, and not the actual decision making power. Questioning around this will help you understand the direction you take after the pitch is closed and you send a proposal.

This is called managing the DMP or decision making process.

Just because you have completed the pitch doesn't mean the job is done. There is going to be a way higher conversion rate if you manage this process correctly.

Now, I would always recommend you ask the right questions at the back end of every pitch to determine how that conversation moves forward, in the next step calendar invite you set. Ideally, you would want a second call with the other parties to join, so you can re-pitch and ask and answer key questions OR you want the first pitched contact to give you access to others to pitch to.

You can only do this by asking the right question so here it is;

In order to understand how best to set up our next conversation, is there anybody else that would be involved in the decision making process moving forward?

This is a nice and clear open question to determine exactly how to move forward, and who with.

Your goal if 'yes', is to bring them together on a next meeting face to face, or conference call over the phone. OR clarify with them that you are able to take forward a one to one conversation with their peer.

Understand clearly where the final decision will come from and always keep the conversation with that person.

The final thing you need is to ensure that the initial person you speak to is on board, and in agreement that they want to move this forward, as if you have that then everything will fall nicely into play, and the opportunity will progress and tend to roll out as it should. If they are not on board, then you have missed something in your pitch, you haven't questioned correctly, created the right deal baby or listened enough.

Be aware with opportunities and be prepared that they blow. Sales Warriors have thick skin they take rejection. But it's not just about being thick-skinned and taking rejection. A true Sales Warrior understands the rejection and why... a majority of the time It's because you missed something. The wrong DM, or you didn't create the deal baby. Question with curiosity and interest. Whatever that may be.

As a Sales Warrior you need to feedback on every opportunity you create to create improvements based on each. This is how you improve and steadily grow and become better and better.

Remember DMP is key to moving conversations forward. The next stage is all-important, because once proposals start to go out you can lose control. So your job is to ensure you understand exactly what needs to happen for their end post pitch to get the decision made. And a big part of your job is ensuring that you assist in doing that.

STAGE 9
Having an Agreement to Move Forward to Proposal and Arranged Call-Back

Closing has a stigma around it. In a nutshell the thoughts around closing are you either you close too soft in that you don't have an agenda, agreement or structure for moving the opportunity to deal; or you close too hard, from which you are over-aggressive, so that you push so much that you lose all the rapport you have built, and you're pushing the customer when they are not ready – it also has a cliché car salesman feel to it. So where do we need to be? Somewhere in the middle is the sweet spot and over the years I have been like a pendulum between the two. But I believe I have finally found that perfect place of closing which has the ability to keep all your hard work intact, keeping that really transparent rapport and relationship building while having a certain class and professionalism to keep you away from being an average car salesman.

The key is to have an agreement in place between you and the customer to either move forward to a deal or to an all-important second conversation, whether that's just with the customer or the DMP. That next step agenda is an agreement between two parties to take the relationship forward and that is very tough for you or the customer to go back on. And it would take something pretty bad to break that agreement.

So that is it. That's what it is all about. It's all about framing these three scenarios at the end of each pitch.

If it's just the customer and no one else is involved and you have answered all his questions and you are at the point of closure:

"So, in effect John, do we have an agreement between us both to move this relationship forward and start working together?"

If there are others in the decision:

"So, in effect John, do we have an agreement between us both to move this relationship forward and set up a next step conversation with you and your colleagues?"

If he needs time to look at the proposal and to think about it:

"So, in effect John, do we have an agreement between us both to move this relationship forward and set up a next step conversation from which I can answer any further questions regards to your thought/proposal?"

These are all you need to take that pitch to opportunity and into proposal - they are the last sentence you say. It's an agreement in place to always be moving the opportunity forward. Whether it books or blows doesn't matter, but you are in control, and that's what does!

You need to then set up a next step agenda which is what is going to happen after that YES. If for example the customer wants to move ahead, you reiterate the procedure of allocation, signature or payment crystal clear, and have that actioned immediately on your terms. He is ready to commit, so you need to finalise and commit the prospect straight away.

If it's a next step conversation to answer questions or promote more material, then you need to explain what the next conversation is for, and pull that together so they want to take a next steps call.

The absolute key afterwards is solidifying that with a meeting in their diaries, confirmed by you there and then, so its rock solid.

As you can see it's all about control and setting and agenda and moving everything forward.

Once you have everything confirmed and you and the customer understand the next steps, and you are happy that there are absolutely no more questions you can answer at this stage, you can procced to your proposal.

Now proposals do not need to be long, lengthy and full of fancy artwork etc. People want the proposal to highlight the key points of your conversation. A proposal needs to be black and white and quickly highlight who you are, what you do, and how you can help them.

Short, sharp, punchy. And gives them quickly a positive image of that picture you painted on your pitch. It's to reignite the excitement levels of your previous conversation and get them back to the point and action threshold on which they want to buy from you, showing how your product can help them achieve their goals.

Backed up though – if you have details you need to send, I always send the detail in an attachment so they have all the information there if they choose to go through it.

The aim of good proposal is this:
- Remind the customer of you, you're the person they are buying from and they need to remember how much they loved you!
- The customed needs to, clearly, in one sentence, remember the core challenges they need to overcome backed up by your solution.
- Any backup info required.
- Package and cost.
- Media kits/Pdf of testimonial/links/all in attachment for him to review after.

That is it! Simple and effective.

On point of calling back, or what is called a call-back: it has to be goal-oriented and objective based. This is where you need in your second call to progress forward to signing and completing your partnership. It's all about withdrawing key questions. What you should be left with in your call back is buying questions which, answered correctly, should be easy enough for you to move to the contract and invoicing.

Unless you have to pitch another DMP or someone else within the process, in which case you go back to start and give them the full picture, as you did the initial DM.

The key to a good call back is about relationship building, trust. You are at the point where you need to do three things
- Isolate any final challenges and questions and overcome them
- Build trust and ensure that the customer is comfortable
- Don't just think about this one deal, think long-term opportunity

Be calm, use the three points as above and then ask for the business partnership.

Congratulations you have closed the deal, but this is only the start of what will be a long-term partnership with huge potential earning opportunities… Only if you manage the process correctly from here.

STAGE 10
Managing that Relationship Forward

Well, congratulations… you have made it to the final stage of Building Sales Warriors. Your journey is nearly at a close.

Your final stage is all about managing that relationship forward. And there are two cardinal sins that I see from sales people that you need to remember – at point of your first agreement with prospect and that is.

- Not connecting with them regularly enough with valuable and helpful support
- Contacting them only when you want more money out of them

The trick is to find a happy medium in between the two. There is an old term of three support contacts before you approach for sale based contact. But to be honest, it is about having regular contact which builds relationships but not friendships, business relationships.

You have to be very careful where you end up as partners as you are in a business relationship. Always remember they are the customer and you are the service supplier. The value, remember, is that you are someone that can help them achieve their goals, and that is real rapport and that needs to continue throughout your relationship.

The key is to continue the relationship after your agreement by having a regular meeting to progress that conversation forward, once every two weeks. But come back with value for them each time, advice, something that can benefit them, something that shows you're always working to help them achieve their goals outside of the product they have paid for.

People say to me, don't do anything for free but you have to look long-term. I started my company based on commission only and also free consultations. Now I'm paid tens of thousands of pounds to help them with their business, because I'm investing my time and my energy to helping them.

It's all about thinking long-term. If you do business on the phone and you have never met the customer I strongly advise you get your arse up and meet them face to face in their office. I would always advise, based on the initial business deal, you have a long-term business meeting to start analysing where you go in the future as partners and what the long-term aspect of your partnership looks like. You need to take them there and begin to build a long-term future plan that is inspiring and excites your client.

It really is just about that relationship that matters, a business relationship where you are vocal about continuing to work with them as partners on their journey to success as partners. And you do that by constantly building value all the way to when perhaps one day which may happen they decide to try something else. And do you know what you still keep that ongoing communication going, constantly bringing opportunity and value to the table, because they will always value it and respect you and that's what relationship selling is all about.

And there you have it… Now I'm not going to sign you off as a Sales Warrior as you ain't until you master the system, so it's in your hands now to get out and work it. It will take time but work it stage by stage and no doubt you will master it.

This book and sales guide is not about detailed sales jargon but a simple structured approach to selling in a way that builds relationships, scales volumes and gets results. I have read hundreds of books in my time and to be honest I get to two chapters in and put them down.. Why? I just get bored. I hope *Building Sales Warriors* has been insightful and more importantly helped you in defining a better outlook and approach to selling. It's worked for me and plenty of others that use my system. And it will work for you. Even if you are a graduate looking to start from scratch and use this system from start to finish then great, or if you are MD that just takes two lines out of book that can help you, it doesn't matter.

Here you have it the secret sauce, the keys to the kingdom and an opportunity to be as successful as you want to be. That's the beauty of sales, all these systems and theories out there don't mean shit unless you are determined to go out and give it everything. It's all about the sales person at the end of the day, and Sales Warriors will always be the first ones up in the morning, on the phone, knocking on doors, sending outreaches, and the last ones to leave the office and shut their laptop down. Thank you so much for coming on this journey with me, and I wish you all the very best for the future!

Dedications &
Acknowledgements

I would like to dedicate this book to my Wife Katie, Son Archie & Daughter Harper. Thankyou for all your support and helping me make this dream a reality.

I wish to acknowledge the influence of Jordan Belfort, who has inspired my own theories and learning and also Dan Gregory who motivated me finally to put pen to paper on this book.

Thank you to Spencer Green who gave me eleven years of support, guidance and experience in my business and sales career.

Finally accreditation for the artwork to Russ Ellingham.

www.ingramcontent.com/pod-product-compliance
Lightning Source LLC
Chambersburg PA
CBHW042047050426
42452CB00019BA/2966